FRIENDS OF THE EARTH

LOUISE SPILSBURY

www.heinemann.co.uk
Visit our website to find out more information about **Heinemann Library** books.

To order:
 Phone 44 (0) 1865 888066
 Send a fax to 44 (0) 1865 314091
 Visit the Heinemann Bookshop at www.heinemann.co.uk to browse our catalogue and order online.

First published in Great Britain by Heinemann Library, Halley Court, Jordan Hill, Oxford OX2 8EJ, a division of Reed Educational and Professional Publishing Ltd. Heinemann is a registered trademark of Reed Educational & Professional Publishing Limited.

OXFORD MELBOURNE AUCKLAND JOHANNESBURG BLANTYRE
GABORONE IBADAN PORTSMOUTH NH (USA) CHICAGO

© Reed Educational and Professional Publishing Ltd 2000.
Published in association with Friends of the Earth. The moral right of the proprietor has been asserted.

Designed by Ken Vail Graphic Design, Cambridge
Originated by Universal Colour Scanning
Printed by Wing King Tong in Hong Kong.

ISBN 0 431 02734 X
04 03 02 01 00
10 9 8 7 6 5 4 3 2 1

Heinemann Library paid a contribution to Friends of the Earth for their help in the creation of this book.

British Library Cataloguing in Publication Data
Spilsbury, Louise
Friends of the Earth. – (Taking Action!)
1.Friends of the Earth – Juvenile literature
I.Title
361.7'63'0941

Acknowledgements
The Publishers would like to thank the following for permission to reproduce photographs:
John Allen/Evening Herald p28 lower right; Adrian Arbib/FOE pp12 right, 13 lower; Jennifer Bates/FOE pp7 upper, 10 all, 11 all, 12 left, 13 upper, 14 all, 15 all, 16 all, 17 all, 18 lower, 19 lower, 20 lower, 21 lower, 25 lower; Nick Cobbing/FOE pp26, 27 lower; Bruce Coleman/Alan Compost p5 upper; Jim Davis/Whitehaven News p7 lower; Environmental Images/Robert Brook p4 lower; Dylan Garcia pp4 upper, 28 left; Nikki Gibbs/FOE pp22 upper, 29 left; Ceanne Jansen/FOE p29 right; Annie Longbottom p23 lower; Maidenhead Advertiser p30; Newsquest North London p8; Bill Osment/FOE p6; Ben Rogers/FOE pp9 upper, 27 upper; Still Pictures p25 upper; Adam Waller/FOE p24; Woodfall Wild Images p5 lower.

All other photos are used courtesy of Friends of the Earth and Friends of the Earth International.

Cover illustration by Scott Rhodes.

Cover photograph by Powerstock Zefa/Sally & Richard Greenhill.

Our thanks to staff at Friends of the Earth for their help in the preparation of this book.

Every effort has been made to contact copyright holders of any material reproduced in this book. Any omissions will be rectified in subsequent printings if notice is given to the Publisher.

Words appearing in the text in bold, **like this**, are explained in the Glossary.

CONTENTS

What's the problem?   4

What does Friends of the Earth do?   6

How does Friends of the Earth work?   8

Meet Liana Stupples – campaigns director   10

Meet Adeela Warley – public
        information manager   12

Meet Chas Linn – web producer   14

Meet Paul de Zylva – campaigns co-ordinator   16

Work in campaigning   18

Work in communications   20

Work by local groups   22

Working around the world   24

The Real Food campaign   26

Tomorrow's world   28

What you can do   30

Glossary   31

Index   32

WHAT'S THE PROBLEM?

We are the problem! Not just you and me, but the 6 billion people who live on this planet, especially those of us who live in the richer countries of the world. Because of the way we treat the planet we are using up the Earth's **natural resources** and one day they will run out!

The world's climate is changing and its forests and natural **habitats** are disappearing. Plants and animals are becoming **extinct** at a faster rate than ever before. Because of **pollution** our air and water are no longer clean and pure. Millions of people all over the world suffer or even die from breathing in filthy air, drinking polluted water and eating **contaminated** food. The natural world and all the living things within it are under threat – and that includes us!

The burning of oil, coal and gas in power stations is causing pollution and is largely to blame for the fact that the climate is changing. Scientists predict more storms, floods, hurricanes, hotter summers, and wetter winters as a result. These changes could bring misery or even death to many people.

Clean water is essential for life. But our rivers and underground water supplies are being threatened by poisons leaking from waste dumps and chemicals from factories and farms, and sewage is polluting some of our best beaches.

Worldwide more than 1000 different species of birds and mammals are now extremely rare.

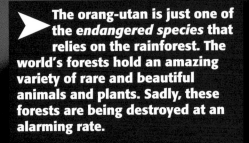

The orang-utan is just one of the *endangered species* that relies on the rainforest. The world's forests hold an amazing variety of rare and beautiful animals and plants. Sadly, these forests are being destroyed at an alarming rate.

The air in many UK cities is not fit to breathe. One in seven children develops *asthma* and up to 24,000 people die every year as a result of air pollution.

Because tropical forests are being destroyed, 27,000 species are made extinct every year.

WHAT DOES FRIENDS OF THE EARTH DO?

How do you treat your friends? Do you treat them with care and consideration? Would you do your best to protect them from things which could harm them? That's how Friends of the Earth thinks we should treat the planet on which we live and its people – like a friend. Since 1971 Friends of the Earth in the UK has been working to protect the **environment** – which is also the best way of ensuring our own future.

ACTING FOR CHANGE

One of Friends of the Earth's jobs is to inform people about environmental problems in the UK and across the world. Friends of the Earth publishes lots of books and leaflets packed with information based on careful research.

Once people are aware of the problems, Friends of the Earth helps them to take action. It may encourage people to make a change themselves, perhaps by cycling to school instead of using a car – or by getting involved in a **campaign**, perhaps by writing to the government to demand changes to laws that protect wildlife.

▲ Waste is a huge problem. Friends of the Earth campaigns for things to be made to last, so they can be *recycled* or reused later. These spoof toys, called 'Trashformers', were used in a campaign at Christmas to show how advertisers persuade children to ask for toys which they don't really need and which don't last.

By getting people to join together in its campaigns, Friends of the Earth can put a lot of pressure on governments and big companies to take action to protect and improve the environment, too.

6

Households in England and Wales throw away 27 million tonnes of waste each year.

To make sure Friends of the Earth gets its facts right, the organization spends almost one-third of its funds on research.

Members of the local group of Friends of the Earth in West Cumbria had great success with this campaign against the build-up of foreign *nuclear waste* in Britain. They used a crazed, giant lobster to bring attention to the issue and to concerns that local seafood was being *contaminated*.

Nearly one in five people in the UK is at risk from dangerous amounts of *pollution*.

HOW DOES FRIENDS OF THE EARTH WORK?

Over the years Friends of the Earth has scored many victories on behalf of the planet. It has saved hundreds of wildlife **habitats**, won protection for **endangered species**, stopped unnecessary and damaging road schemes, blocked unsafe plans for **nuclear waste** dumping and in 1998 alone achieved the passing of five **Acts of Parliament**, to name but a few. How does Friends of the Earth do it?

HOME AND AWAY

Friends of the Earth works at all levels – locally, nationally and internationally. In the UK alone, Friends of the Earth has a network of local groups working in more than 200 communities throughout England, Wales and Northern Ireland. These groups are supported by full-time workers at the head office in London, as well as five English regional offices and offices in Wales and Northern Ireland. With over 60 national groups across five continents, Friends of the Earth is also one of the biggest international **environmental** networks in the world.

▲ Another success! These Friends of the Earth supporters are enjoying a well-earned glass of champagne. After a 10-year *campaign*, local groups managed to halt plans to widen London's North Circular Road.

There are now around 500 million cars *polluting* the planet.

MONEY MATTERS

Friends of the Earth depends on the money its supporters send in to carry out all its research and campaigns. Over nine-tenths of its funds come from ordinary people who want to see Friends of the Earth achieve its aims and improve the environment in which we live. Friends of the Earth also sells environmentally friendly products by mail through its **trading partner**, Natural Collection.

▶ **Every success that Friends of the Earth achieves is a result of the work made possible by supporters who give money to the organization.**

▼ **Friends of the Earth International (FOEI) works with people and communities around the world to help them in their battles against threats to their local environments. This is a Friends of the Earth ('Amigos da Terra') *demonstration* in Brazil.**

The UK *recycles* only 8% of its household waste. The Netherlands recycles 60%.

MEET LIANA STUPPLES

CAMPAIGNS DIRECTOR

I am **campaigns** director at Friends of the Earth's London office. It's my job to help spread the word about what Friends of the Earth is doing, and to help organize campaigns all over the country.

I like my job because I get to talk to all sorts of people from all over the country and across the world. In one day I might talk to a government **minister** about new wildlife laws; a businesswoman about her company's **environmental** policies; a supporter from Brazil with news about what is going on there; a concerned parent wanting to stop a farmer growing **GM** crops near their home; and do a radio interview about an issue that's in the news!

I always ride my mountain bike to work. Some people think I must be crazy to cycle in London. But it's the fastest way to get around – and it's fun!

8.45am When I get to work I read through my e-mails. I get about 100 a day from Friends of the Earth staff, local groups around the country and other campaigners all over the world.

10am At a **media** meeting with the other campaign workers from the office we talk about the previous week's news stories and what campaigns are coming up. We plan the best ways of getting newspapers and TV to do reports about important environmental issues, and prepare well-researched information sheets they can use.

Climate change **meant that 1998 was the world's**

11am I check through an early version of a leaflet we are producing about food issues, part of a campaign to improve the choice and quality of the food people eat. While doing this I also take calls from lots of people, including a minister who wants to discuss our ideas for new laws to protect wildlife.

2pm After lunch, ITV want me to do an interview about a new government scheme for **green energy**. I talk to our energy campaigner to make sure my facts are up-to-date before biking over to the TV station for the interview.

4pm Back to my desk to put together some notes for a talk I'm giving this evening. The meeting is with some business people about how companies could behave more responsibly towards the environment. It starts at 5.30 and goes on for a long time because everyone wants to talk about the issues I've raised, which is great.

At our media meeting today we talk about campaigns on *nuclear waste* and new research showing that factories which cause *pollution* are much more likely to be built in areas where poorer people live.

Often when I talk to a group of people from business they are surprised by how much research I have done into the money side of their industries. Friends of the Earth knows it's important to be aware of how companies can save money by being more environmentally friendly.

Modern farming methods have caused a serious
decline in some bird populations

MEET ADEELA WARLEY

PUBLIC INFORMATION MANAGER

Have you ever picked up a free postcard about Friends of the Earth at the cinema? If the answer is yes, the chances are I helped get it displayed there. As public information manager it's part of my job to find ways to draw people's attention to our **campaigns**.

I also write practical guides and leaflets which help people take action, I talk to journalists and I work with the design team to come up with advertising posters and create our website.

Today we are launching 'London – The Living City', an **environmental** poetry show for some of London's busiest bus routes. We asked people to write about what they loved about their local environment or how it could be improved.

7.00am Off by train to Covent Garden, in the West End of London, where photographers from the **media** are going to take pictures of the poets.

9.00am Our red London buses have arrived; the celebrity and prizewinning poets are all there and so are the TV and newspaper photographers. BBC Radio 4 records a special feature for their programme 'Woman's Hour'.

Celebrity poets including John Hegley, Roger McGough and Benjamin Zephaniah contributed poems, and hundreds of budding poets of all ages entered our competition to get their poem displayed on a London bus.

Cle

11.00am Time for a break. We all go inside the London Transport Museum for a tea party. This is our chance to say a big thank you to the many people who helped make the project such a success.

12.00 noon Out on the Covent Garden Piazza, performance poet John Citizen and I do a broadcast with Radio 5 Live. It's great to know this is helping us spread our message to thousands of Londoners.

3.00pm All aboard! We take the competition winners on a special bus trip and the surprise destination is St. James's Church, Piccadilly. For me, this is the most magical part of the day as the poets read their winning poems, gathered around the font where the great poet William Blake was christened in 1757.

▼ **Our 'Poetry on the buses' campaign is a great way to get people thinking about the environment – as well as making their journeys more fun.**

▼ **It's great to have a chance to do radio interviews about the poetry day. Lots of people will hear about Friends of the Earth and hopefully want to find out more about our campaigns.**

4.30pm I make a few last calls to newspapers to make sure stories about this special event appear in as many papers and magazines as possible. Then I head back to the office to think about this brilliant day.

Some vegetables have been found to contain 20 times the legal limits of pesticide traces.

MEET CHAS LINN

WEB PRODUCER

My job title makes me sound like a giant spider! Actually, I run Friends of the Earth's huge internet website. I collect all the information we show on the site to make sure that all the people who look at it can find out the information they need to live safe, healthy and **environmentally** friendly lives.

Working on the website is very exciting because your work is seen immediately by over 2000 people every day. This is great when everything goes well, but it's terrible when you make mistakes – just imagine your spelling mistakes being seen not only by your teacher but by an audience of thousands, many of whom can't wait to tell you about them!

This is a page from Friends of the Earth's **Factory Watch website. The site makes it fast and simple for people to get the facts on the factories that are *polluting* their neighbourhood. You can visit this website at www.foe.co.uk/factorywatch.**

9am My first job of the day is to check my e-mails. I get about 50 a day with all sorts of messages about the website. They range from people wanting to become members, to very exotic requests from foreign countries — once someone from Brazil asked me about building a cathedral made from plants in the jungle!

10.30am I speak to our art director about our new food website. We decide to use some wonderful pictures of strawberries and apples on the front page.

11.30am I meet our computer programmers to discuss creating some clever new games for our website. One of our most important creations this year has been an internet machine which tells readers all about factories which pollute the environment. It is called Factory Watch and it has been really successful — it even won second place in the charity website of the year awards, which was very exciting.

▲ The computer programmer and I try out some of the new games we have devised for the website.

1.30pm Time to sort out some website pages. Producing all the pages on our website takes a lot of time. Sometimes there are five of us at work putting all the information and pictures in the right place and checking they are all clear.

▼ Every year factories pump tonnes of dangerous chemicals into our air. This pollution threatens our health. Friends of the Earth's Factory Watch *campaign* aims to give people the facts they need to take action to stop pollution in their own neighbourhoods.

4.30pm I speak to journalists about our new website, persuading them to tell the rest of the world how useful and interesting it is. This is important because we really need to tell people about what we do, so that they can go on to help the environment themselves.

Friends of the Earth has uncovered the location of thousands of *toxic* waste dumps.

MEET PAUL DE ZYLVA
CAMPAIGNS CO-ORDINATOR

My name is Paul and I am London **campaigns** co-ordinator for Friends of the Earth. My job is to help people organize their campaigns more effectively. I also help with Friends of the Earth's work on the bigger issues that threaten the local **environment**, such as plans to expand Heathrow Airport.

One of the things I like about my job is that I get to meet people face to face to help them with their problems. I also give talks to groups and schools about Friends of the Earth. It's great to hear what people like you think about what Friends of the Earth does.

7am I'm up early for a Breakfast Show radio interview about air **pollution**, children's health and traffic in London. We are in the news because we are organizing a public meeting in Greenwich tomorrow about the terrible amount of traffic there.

9am Back at the office I check my telephone and e-mail messages.

10am I write a press release for tomorrow's meeting. This is a sheet of information which I send out to the **media** to encourage them to write or broadcast news about particular events or issues.

Friends of the Earth supports campaigners like these who want to stop the building of a fifth terminal at London's Heathrow Airport. There are fears that a new runway may also be built, which would increase noise and air pollution in the area.

Traffic fumes contain some of the most harmful

12 noon I answer calls from journalists who have received the press releases and want to cover the story in their newspapers or arrange interviews for their radio or TV shows. I also speak to a teacher about giving a talk to her school.

2pm I go to a meeting with a community group about a plan to build homes on some old factory land. They fear the land is **contaminated** and that it is not safe to build houses there.

4.30pm I do a final check on the equipment we need for tomorrow night's meeting — slides, projector, screen, leaflets, etc...

7pm I head off to an evening meeting with our local group in Hackney to help them plan their events and work over the next six months. I get home at midnight after another busy and exciting day!

▼ **I put up posters at the building site where local people fear the land is contaminated. If we can draw enough attention to their concerns, a proper investigation should take place.**

▼ **Meetings with Friends of the Earth local groups are usually lively and fun. Most campaigners are full of ideas for things they want to do to improve their local environment.**

About 2000 people in London die each year because of poor air quality.

WORK IN CAMPAIGNING

Governments and big companies make decisions and take actions which can have extremely harmful effects on the **environment** in the UK and all over the world. One of Friends of the Earth's most important jobs is to get people to join together in **campaigns** to make their voices heard. When people take action together they can persuade governments to make laws to protect the environment and encourage businesses to find positive solutions to the environmental problems their industries create.

Each year many wild places in the UK are ploughed up, drained, or concreted over for roads or buildings. The plants and animals living in them will die out if their homes are damaged. Friends of the Earth is campaigning in lots of different ways to save these wild places.

WORKING FOR CHANGE

Working to persuade **ministers** or bosses of big companies to make important changes to the way they do things is an important part of campaigning. Friends of the Earth spends a lot of time and effort on researching the facts surrounding the issues it campaigns on so its representatives are well-informed and well-prepared.

These Friends of the Earth supporters are outside *Parliament* demanding a new wildlife law. This would mean much stronger protection for wildlife and their *habitats* all over the UK.

Energy-saving lightbulbs pay for themselves four times over in saved electricity costs.

Wild Places Under Threat!
You can help protect them...

ring 0171 490 1555
to order a free Wild Places! Information Pack
connect to the Wild Places!
pages on Friends of the Earth's website
http// www.foe.co.uk/wildplaces

WILDPLACES

FRIENDS *of the*
earth

Over 300 of our most important Wild Places are damaged each year – we can't afford to lose them.

◄ **Posters like this tell people about the dangers affecting wild places in the UK – and how they can take action!**

Friends of the Earth also uses all sorts of other methods to make its campaigns succeed. It organizes peaceful protests or **demonstrations**, sometimes outside Parliament if an important law is being discussed. It uses eye-catching publicity stunts, leaflets, adverts and posters to inform people and persuade them to add their support to its campaigns.

▼ **Simple actions like sending a letter saying what you think can make a difference. When thousands of letters on an issue are delivered to the Prime Minister's letterbox, he is likely to take notice.**

Every year over 300 of the UK's most important wild places are damaged.

WORK IN COMMUNICATIONS

How do you find out about what is going on in your town, your country or even the world? You read newspapers or magazines, listen to the radio, watch TV or search the internet. These forms of communication are known as the **media**. Friends of the Earth uses the media in lots of different ways to inform people about **environmental** issues and to tell them what they can do to help.

READ ALL ABOUT IT!

Friends of the Earth believes people can only be ready to work for change when they are armed with the facts. Friends of the Earth publishes a wide range of leaflets, posters, booklets, reports and other kinds of information. They cover a variety of issues, ranging from air **pollution** to saving tropical rainforests. And they come in lots of different forms, from leaflets aimed at children to technical reports aimed at government officials. Friends of the Earth even has its own website (www.foe.co.uk) which offers some publications free of charge.

▲ Friends of the Earth's magazine, *Earth Matters*, contains articles on current *campaigns*, news items, book reviews, information about environmental issues around the world, suggestions for taking action and a children's section, KM.

▶ People phone up Friends of the Earth to ask about all sorts of things – from how many wild cats are left in the UK, to how to organize a *demonstration* against a new road being built in their area.

Friends of the Earth handles over 30,000 requests for information every year.

MAKING HEADLINES

Getting environmental issues into the news is a vital part of Friends of the Earth's work. When a topic has been researched, press releases are sent out to the media. These are sheets of background information around which journalists base their stories. Journalists may also ring the Friends of the Earth office to ask for information about an issue that is in the news or that they want to write about.

Friends of the Earth often uses gimmicks to grab people's attention and get issues into the news. Sometimes it may ask someone famous to join a particular campaign to get more people to support it.

Famous people sometimes help to draw people's attention to a cause. Here comedian Ben Elton is speaking in support of Friends of the Earth's 'Fuming Mad' campaign to reduce traffic in the UK.

If you ever want to know about an environmental issue, Friends of the Earth's booklets give you the facts.

Out of every £75 spent on groceries, £10 is for the packaging – which is almost all thrown away.

WORK BY LOCAL GROUPS

An **incinerator** is stopped from being built in Manchester; a wind farm gets planning permission in Southport; plans for a gigantic landfill dump are rejected in Northern Ireland; boxes of **organic** food are sold all over Maidenhead. All over the UK Friends of the Earth local groups are taking action and making changes like these. There are more than 200 Friends of the Earth local groups with around 10,000 members in England, Wales and Northern Ireland.

Campaigner Cathy Maguire is fighting plans for a *toxic* waste dump near her home in West Belfast, Northern Ireland.

Local groups may focus their attentions on an issue which only directly affects the people living in their area – such as a new road scheme which threatens a local natural **habitat**. They may call on the head office for advice, but they will **campaign** and organize **demonstrations** for themselves. But local groups are also involved in national and international campaigns, such as those to stop dangerous **climate change**.

Friends of the Earth publishes a magazine for local groups called *Change Your World*. It keeps members up to date on issues, advises on campaigns and gives tips on how to make local groups more effective.

22

Over 1350 rubbish dumps in the UK are at risk of leaking poisons and damaging water supplies.

◄ A young supporter from the Friends of the Earth local group in Portsmouth collected a huge weight of rubbish when she helped clear up the local beaches.

▼ Supporters from the Friends of the Earth local group in Leeds used a giant weather map of the UK to show how the country will suffer severe weather changes due to climate change if action is not taken.

Recycling one tonne of steel saves 0.9 tonnes of raw materials.

WORKING AROUND THE WORLD

Thinking globally, acting locally is what Friends of the Earth supporters in local groups across the UK do. They know that **campaigns** they support in their own home towns can affect the **environment** across the world. The international branch of the organization, Friends of the Earth International (FOEI), works with people and communities around the world to help them in their battles with local threats to the environment. This international network includes nearly 60 national groups across five continents who work together on important environmental issues.

MAHOGANY IS MURDER!

In 1992 Friends of the Earth campaigners in Brazil asked supporters in the UK to persuade people in Britain to stop buying furniture made from mahogany wood. Cutting down rainforests for mahogany has terrible effects on the Amazon environment and the animals and people who live there.

One of Friends of the Earth International's biggest campaigns is against *climate change*. In this picture supporters stage a *demonstration* to persuade world leaders like US president Bill Clinton to improve international laws and to stop 'cooking the world'.

The loss of rainforests is also a disaster for people all over the world. These forests play an important role in controlling our climate and their loss is contributing to dangerous changes to the world's climate. Also many scientists believe that they may contain plants which could provide helpful treatments or even cures for some life-threatening diseases.

An area of tropical rainforest larger than England and Wales is destroyed every year.

FROM THE DRAGON'S TAIL

'Dragon's tail' is the name of a strip of mountainous forest sandwiched between Laos and Vietnam in South-east Asia. These forests and the people and wildlife who live there are fighting for survival. In 1970, Cambodia's forests covered three-quarters of the country's land – now they cover less than a third. To halt this destruction, the sale of Cambodian timber abroad was banned in 1996. However, it is now being bought by Vietnamese companies who pretend it is from their own country. This timber is made into garden furniture and sold to garden centres in Europe. By making people aware of crimes like these, Friends of the Earth hopes to stop trade in illegal timber and save the world's precious forests.

The clearing of the Amazonian rainforests is robbing many people, including this Yanomami boy from Venezuela, of their homes.

A Friends of the Earth campaigner is interviewed about the campaign to stop UK shops like Argos selling Vietnamese garden furniture.

Scientists believe climate change causes some natural disasters, such as hurricanes.

THE REAL FOOD CAMPAIGN

We all want to eat food that tastes good, which is safe and healthy and does not spoil the **environment**. However, many of the ways in which food is being produced today are not good – not for farm animals, wildlife, the environment, and certainly not for us.

Many farms use vast amounts of artificial chemicals to grow their crops. Many of these kill butterflies, birds and flowers and **pollute** the soil, rivers, and even the crops we eat. To increase the amount of food that farms can produce, animals are often kept in unnatural and sometimes cruel ways. Friends of the Earth is **campaigning** to change all this and to bring back 'real' food.

ORGANIC FARMING

Organic farms grow crops and raise animals without using artificial chemicals. Instead, farmers use compost and manure from farm animals to feed the land, and other plants and insects to control **pests**. Animals kept on organic farms are allowed to roam outside instead of being kept in pens for long periods of time. Many people believe that food grown organically tastes better and is safer to eat than food which may be polluted with chemicals.

Big, out-of-town supermarkets are often built on precious countryside, take business away from smaller local shops and encourage people to use their cars more. In Veggie box schemes like this one, farmers deliver boxes of fresh vegetables to local customers at home.

Worldwide, 800 million people are ill because they don't eat enough nourishing food.

GM FOODS

GM (genetically modified) foods are completely new kinds of food. They are created by scientists who take **genes** from one living thing and put them into another. This creates plants and animals which would never occur naturally. Companies do this to make crops that can survive being sprayed with harmful chemicals like **pesticides**, and to make food stay fresher longer. The problem is that no one knows what effects GM food could have on the environment or on our health.

Friends of the Earth is campaigning to stop the production of GM foods until they have been properly tested, and to remove all GM foods from our shops.

▲ **Friends of the Earth's 'Genebeast' monster toured the country's supermarkets to remind managers about shoppers' concern over GM foods.**

▶ **Friends of the Earth is calling for a five-year 'freeze' on the growth and sale of GM food. This would give scientists time to study the long-term effects of eating and growing GM food.**

27

All the big supermarkets are now banning GM ingredients from their own food products.

TOMORROW'S WORLD

At the moment the rich, developed world is using a much larger share of the Earth's **natural resources** than the developing world. Friends of the Earth believes that everyone has the right to a fair share of the Earth's resources and that the needs of everyone on the planet can be met if we all use those resources carefully and fairly. This would lead to an improvement in everyone's quality of life. It would protect our health, create new jobs for the millions of unemployed people across the world, and create a fairer world. Looking after the planet is also the best way of looking after people.

We look forward to a world where natural *habitats* and wildlife are saved and protected.

In the future all the world's children will be protected from poverty and *pollution* and the illnesses both those problems can create.

More of the power we use will come from *green energy* sources like the wind or sun. These wind turbines make power using the energy of the wind.

▲ Traffic will be cut as more people use bikes, buses and trains to get around. Shops will be nearer our homes instead of out-of-town.

▲ There will be tasty *organic* food for all!

▲ People and industry will waste less and there will be huge increases in the amount of waste which is *recycled*.

WHAT YOU CAN DO

Friends of the Earth needs help with a whole range of **campaigns**, from better protection for wildlife to **green energy**. To find out how you can help, or for more information on any **environmental** issue, write to:

Friends of the Earth
26–28 Underwood Street
London N1 7JQ.
Or contact Friends of the Earth on e-mail at:
info@foe.co.uk
There is also lots of information available on Friends of the Earth's website at: www.foe.co.uk

There are also five simple, everyday things you can do to help the environment.

1 Use less paper and always try to buy **recycled** paper products. Encourage your school to do so, too.
2 Refuse to take unnecessary packaging when you buy anything. Reuse things like envelopes, bags and containers – get your family to recycle as much as they can at home. If there aren't enough recycling facilities, ask your council to provide more.
3 Take showers instead of baths. Use your washing-up water on your plants! Write to your water company to urge them to stop wasting water.
4 Walk, cycle and use public transport whenever possible. Let your local MP know you want him/her to support plans to reduce traffic.
5 Get your family to replace its three most-used lightbulbs with low-energy lightbulbs. Write to the company that supplies your electricity asking what they are doing to develop cleaner energy sources and help your household save energy.

▷ These children are taking action! Instead of being driven to school, they are joining a 'walking bus', organized by the Maidenhead Friends of the Earth local group. Two or three parents gradually pick up more and more children as they get closer to school, walking in a chain. It's a safe and environmentally friendly way to start the day.

GLOSSARY

Act of Parliament law made by Parliament

asthma condition which causes wheezing and difficulty in breathing. Asthma attacks are usually mild, but can be more serious.

campaign activity to bring about change

climate change heating up of the world's climate, and increase in violent weather such as hurricanes. It is caused by pollution of the atmosphere, especially by burning fossil fuels.

contaminated polluted or poisoned

demonstration group of people coming together to show how strongly they feel about something

endangered species plant or animal in danger of becoming extinct

environment/environmental the surroundings in which we and other living creatures live, like seas, rivers, forests, air, or buildings

extinct describes a life form which has died out

genes information in all living things that determines the way they are

GM genetically modified. GM crops are plants which have been altered in some way by adding or taking away certain genes.

green energy energy sources like sun, wind or water power which are much less harmful to the environment than fossil fuels

habitats natural places where plants and animals live

incinerator furnace for burning huge amounts of waste

media newspapers, magazines, radio, television, satellite and other forms of communication

ministers politicians who are chosen to work in the government

natural resources useful things produced by the Earth, including water, wood and minerals

nuclear waste very dangerous waste from nuclear power stations

organic type of farming which does not use artificial chemicals

Parliament elected body of politicians who make our country's laws

pesticide chemical used to kill or control insects on crops and weeds in fields

pests insects or animals which damage or destroy crops

pollute/pollution poisoning or harming any part of the environment

recycle use materials or things again

toxic poisonous

trading partners companies which do business together

31

INDEX

Acts of Parliament 8, 31

climate change 4, 10, 22, 23, 24, 25, 31

demonstrations 19, 20, 22, 24, 31

endangered species 5, 8, 31
energy 31

factories 4, 14, 15
farming 11, 26
Friends of the Earth International 8, 9, 24
fund-raising 9

GM food 10, 27, 31
governments 6, 18
green energy 11, 28, 30, 31

habitats 4, 8, 18, 22, 28, 31
Heathrow Airport 16

laws 6, 10, 11, 18, 24
local groups 7, 8, 17, 22, 23, 24

mail-order sales 9
media 10, 11, 12, 16, 20, 21, 31

nuclear waste 7, 8, 11, 31

organic food 22, 26, 29, 31

Parliament 8, 18, 19, 31
pesticides 12, 13, 27, 31
pollution 4, 5, 7, 8, 11, 14, 15, 16, 20, 26, 28, 31
posters 19
poverty 28
publications 6, 20, 21
publicity 6, 12, 19, 21

rainforests 5, 20, 24, 25
recycling 6, 9, 29, 30, 31
research 6, 7, 9, 18, 21

toxic waste 15, 22, 31
traffic 6, 8, 16, 21, 29, 30
Trashformer toys 6

Veggie box schemes 26

waste 6, 9, 15, 21, 29
water 4, 12, 22, 30
website 12, 14, 15, 20, 30